Your Words

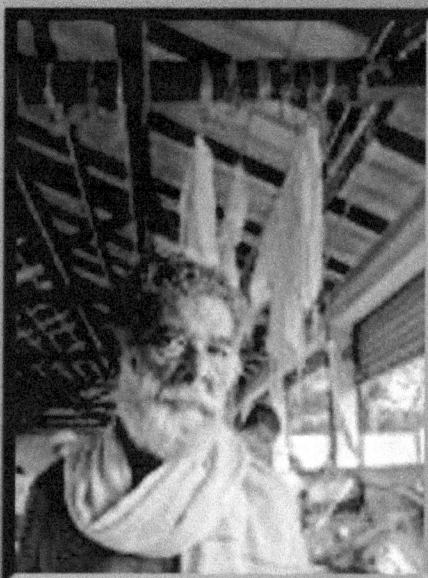

By: Winner Torborg

Your Words

"By your words you will be declared innocent, or by your words you will be declared guilty," (Matthew 12:47 GOD'S WORD Translation)

By: Winner Torborg

Bread of Life International Ministries

Credentials

Almost all his life people around
Winner have been trying to get the best of him.
Winner was always the kind of guy who, if he
found a good cause, would do he best to help.
He was never one for falsity although he did
have a hard time catching others in their lies.

In September of 1980, Winner Torborg
made the life changing confession that Jesus is
Lord; he was at the age of 19 years at the time.
Four years later, September of 1984, at a
Christian meeting Winner asked for and
received the anointing of the Holy Spirit; right
then everything he had read in the Bible came
alive to him and his ability to learn and grasp
knowledge of God's Word increased mightily.
The next day he answered the call of God to step
into the ministry, mainly as a teacher.

As a teacher, Winner had to learn and
retain knowledge from the Bible and from
watching how other people act in their lives. In
September of 1985, Winner began a newsletter
ministry called Bread of Life. He started by
writing to a group of church people, and his

ministry grew. In 1997, Winner put his ministry on the World Wide Web, and the name changed to Bread of Life International Ministries. He is now reaching people from all around the world in many different languages.

Winner also writes for many online magazines and for Bread of Life International Ministries (www.bolim.org).

Why I use many versions of the Bible?

I do this because there is not one version that has every verse right; none of the modern versions have been translated directly from the original Hebrew, Aramaic and Greek. If I only used the King James you would get only a King James approach to God's Word; likewise, if I only used the NIV you would get an NIV approach. I want to share the clearest approach that I can so I must use many versions. As an ancient saying that many people claim as their own goes, "There is more than one way to go up a mountain." I use many Bibles but you must let the Holy Spirit guide you. And I suggest that you get many versions also. In one version a verse may be quoted one way and in another the same verse is quoted a totally different way.

A good example of this is Romans 8:28; in the King James Version and some others versions it says one thing and in the NIV and some other versions it says another. But, Paul is talking about prayer things in verses 26-29. If you were to add the word 'prayer' into verse 28 you could see that they are both saying the same thing.

Your Words
Table of Contents

Your Words
Prologue

There is such a recklessness going around the world when it comes to using words; Christians using their words recklessly and thinking that their words don't affect or have an effect on anyone, that it's God's Words that count. Well, in a sense that is true, it is God's Words that you make to be your words that count. When you take God's Words and put them into your mouth and speak them then they are your words.

On the other hand, if you are speaking words that the devil said, those words also become your words.

Many people have complained to me that so-n-so said some bad things to them, things they wouldn't repeat; or called them ugly names. I would always tell them that those words that so-n-so said, that the person did not repeat, well those words are so-n-so's, and it is so-n-so's words that will either justify or condemn so-n-so; not condemn the person who wouldn't repeat those words.

Let me give you an example: Jill and Bob were associates. Jill didn't like the way that Bob was handling things so she pulled him aside and said some pretty dog gone rude things to him, things that Bob wouldn't repeat even if asked. Bob came to me and told me that Jill was saying some pretty rotten things to him and he wasn't going to repeat them. I told Bob that those words were Jill's words and not his, so if he didn't allow them, they would have no effect on him. But, those words will have an effect in her life.

Earlier I had written a book called *The Echo Effect* with 2 sections; one called Say What? and the other called The Greatest Weapons Ever Heard. This Book goes right along with that book; it is, in other words, a sequel to that book.

Many doctors have come to the realization that people's words can affect and have a definite effect on their health. People's words can have an effect on more than their health. How about on their social standing, their finances, you name it?

Your Words

Chapter 1
The Word Works

"And God said, "Let there be light," and there was light," (Genesis 1:3 New International Version).

How did God create the world? He said things and they became reality; actually, they were reality as soon as God said them and they became something that *we* call reality. Someone will probably argue, "He said them but then the Spirit did them." You are so right. But God's Spirit never did anything without God *or* His people saying it *first*.

"Then God said, 'Let us make human beings in our image, to be like us. They will reign over the fish in the sea, the birds in the sky, the

> livestock, all the wild animals on the
> earth, and the small animals that scurry
> along the ground,'" (Genesis 1:26 New
> Living Translation).

We have authority over the peeps (fish), the cheeps (birds), the sheep (animals and livestock) and the creeps. So, man was created to be like (approximating) God, that means nearly exactly like God. Now, there is no way, in the physical, that we can look like God since God is the Spirit. But, did you know that we can sound like Him? Not in pitch or tone but in speech. Indeed, that is the image that He created us in; it wasn't the physical image of the Spirit, there is none, but it was the verbal image of the Spirit of God.

There is someone else in Genesis 3 who used words to tempt,

> "But the serpent said to the
> woman, You shall not surely die,"
> (Genesis 3:4 Amplified Bible).

But either way you use words they will work. God's Words were used to create; yes, I know, the Spirit of God worked upon His words. The devil (the serpent) also used words, but he/it used them to deceive; he/it perverted words but they still had their effect.

Now, there is one whom God created who has a God given right to choose either to copy the words of God or the words of the devil; that one is a human. That's right, God created you and He created you to speak like Him. But He gave you an inalienable right—a God given right—when He created you. That right is to choose whom you are going to speak like, the creator or the perverter. Either way, those words that you speak have creative power and they will work. If you speak words of negativity, the power behind those words will work negativity *in your life*. On the other hand, if you speak words of positivity, the power behind those words will work positivity *in your life*.

Yes, you guessed it, you have the choice whether you are going to speak negative words or positive words. Making this choice is so simple that people do it without thinking, but then eventually those words will take an effect in their *own* lives. But, I will show you a better way; before you decide what words you are going to say think for a second or a minute if you can and ask yourself, "Now, what do I want to happen in my *own* life?" If your answer is "positive things" then that is how you should speak.

Now, whether you are speaking over your own life or speaking into someone else's life your words will be the same.

> "The entire law is summed up in a single command: 'Love your neighbor as yourself,'" (Galatians 5:14 New International Version).

For this exercise let's change the word **love** to **speak to**; to love someone you are going to want to speak to them. So, let's use it that way, "The entire law is summed up in a single command: 'Speak to your neighbor as yourself.'" How would you speak to yourself? How would you speak over or about yourself? Remember, God created you to be like Him. Do you think God would talk down about Himself? Well, that other person is also created to be like God.

Whose Words?

> "For by your words you will be acquitted, and by your words you will be condemned," (Matthew 12:37 New International Version).

A while ago as I was studying and praying about my book called *The Echo Effect*

God brought my attention to this verse. I was reading the passage from 12:34-37 and God highlighted verse 37 in my eyes. Allow me to show you,

> "For by **your** (*own*) words **you** will be acquitted, and by **your** (*own*) words **you** will be condemned."

But you will probably come up with this excuse, "Yea, but they are not my words, I just repeated them." God and the devil author words; God authors positive, uplifting, productive words and the devil authors a perverted version of those words which turn out negative, worrisome, and destructive. There are many ways that these words can come to you, called signs. But when they come out of *your* mouth they become *your* words. You see, just because they go in your ears or eyes doesn't make them your words, not until you agree with and possess them. And how do you agree with and possess them? You agree with what they say by saying what they say and that is how you make their words your words.

The verse just before that one, verse 36, says,

> "But I say unto you, That every idle word that men shall speak, they shall give account thereof in the

day of judgment," (King James Version).

Now, this is how the Lord explained it to me; words are active—all words. There is no such thing as a word that doesn't do anything; you can see that when you form a sentence with your words, each word has its part. So, since every word is active, it is either a positive (productive) word or a negative (destructive) word. Now, you are going to be judged for every word that you speak, meaning they will manifest in your life sometime. Now, since that is true, wouldn't you want to be judged for positive (uplifting, productive) words rather than for negative (worrisome, destructive) words?

I asked the Lord about when the day of judgment is. It is not necessarily the last of the last days when Jesus comes back, although that is 1 definition. When something bad happens to someone and they wind up in a hospital, I've heard people say, "They are being judged for something they did." When a tornado takes a church away or wrecks someone's house they say that they are just being judged. Those are judgment days but they are not the last day when Jesus is coming back, they are simply manifestation days in which people will give an account.

Myself, I used to sing along with a stupid song, and 4 to 8 years later was the judgment day for that, I wound up in the hospital, under the knife, and when I woke up I had exactly what I was singing. Now, here is Matthew 12:34-37 from The Message;

> "You have minds like a snake pit! How do you suppose what you say is worth anything when you are so foul-minded? It's your heart, not the dictionary, that gives meaning to your words. A good person produces good deeds and words season after season. An evil person is a blight on the orchard. Let me tell you something: Every one of these careless words is going to come back to haunt you. There will be a time of Reckoning. Words are powerful; take them seriously. Words can be your salvation. Words can also be your damnation."

That's one reason why Jesus said,

> "bless those who curse you, pray for those who mistreat you," (Luke 8:26 New International Version).

When you bless a person you are not speaking destructive words to them, about them, or over them; when they curse you they are doing that to you with their words. Always remember,

> "Here is a simple, rule-of-thumb guide for behavior: Ask yourself what you want people to do for you, then grab the initiative and do it for them. Add up God's Law and Prophets and this is what you get," (Matthew 7:12 The Message).

If you are going to do it then you must be willing to speak it also. So, change the word **do** to the word **speak** and let's read that again.

> "Here is a simple, rule-of-thumb guide for behavior: Ask yourself what you want people to **speak** for you, then grab the initiative and **speak** it for them. Add up God's Law and Prophets and this is what you get."

Chapter 2
Receive it or Not

The verse that used to stick out to me most is Proverbs 18:21,

> "The tongue has the power of life and death, and those who love it will eat its fruit," (New International Version).

This told me that whether you are speaking over yourself or others your words can either be death words or life words. And either way, whether you're speaking over yourself or someone else you yourself will reap from those words. You have probably heard someone say something along the lines of "eat your words." Well, that verse is where that phrase originated from; the fruit of your tongue is words. And, of course, for those who still don't understand; when talking about words being the fruit of your tongue we are talking about the results of the words or the manifestation, when your words actually take on a physical attribute in your life.

But then I ran across a verse that Jesus Himself said,

> "For by your words you will be justified and acquitted, and by your words you will be condemned and sentenced," (Matthew 12:37 Amplified Bible).

I asked The Lord about that verse, I asked Jesus to clarify. He did, He told me that it is by my _own_ words that I will be justified and acquitted, and by my _own_ words I will be condemned and sentenced.

In other words, you shouldn't try to depend on someone else to justify you, not in God's sight; and no one else can condemn you, not in the sight of God. Other people can speak and give you justification, and I'm not talking about excuses for doing something wrong; or they can speak and try—whether knowingly or not—to condemn you; but not before God. As the Bible says,

> "Who are you to pass judgment on and censure another's household servant? It is before his own master that he stands or falls. And he shall stand and be upheld, for the Master (the Lord) is mighty to support him and make him stand," (Romans 14:4 Amplified Bible).

In that verse the question is what I want you to look at. You have no right to talk down about and condemn anyone, especially if he doesn't work for you.

Do you remember those things—I think they were called Pitch-backs—those, sort of, net-type trampolines on their sides? I had one back in the 1970's. I would pitch a ball at it and it would rebound the ball to me so I could catch it. Anyway, when you say something about someone think of the transaction with your words as a Pitch-back. The only thing different is that when you pitch the word it rebounds and comes straight at you. Think of your words as heat-seeking missiles (these heat-seekers are trained on the speaker and you can't shake them), and they will return to you whether the other person receives them or not.

If you are on the mountain and those other guys are in the valley it's not right for you to condemn them because they are in the valley. You might get mad and say, "Oh, those guys in the valley, they're so stupid..." and you go on ranting and raving about those guys in the valley. In the first place, you don't have the right to speak that way because they are not your servants. And another thing is that you will be in the valley soon and they may be on the mountain.

> "So whatever you wish that others would do to you, do also to them, for this is the Law and the Prophets," (Matthew 7:12 English Standard Version).

In this verse you could easily, and this would be right also, substitute the word **say** for **do**. What are the things that you would have people say unto you or to speak into your life? If you want others to speak negatively into your life, to you or about you then speak negatively to or about anyone whom you feel hurt you.

They are all God's creation; so, if you are speaking negatively over one of God's creation, what are you saying about the One who created God's creation? If you say to a man whom God created to be a man, he is well into his thirties, forties or fifties, "You're a sissy girl!" Did you just insult that man's creator?

Remember, those words will rebound to you. You have no right to judge them but you can judge their actions. He might be acting like a sissy girl but he is still a man whom God created.

It might not have a lasting effect in your life when people judge you but, I guarantee, it does hurt. I had people judge me and I heard or read their judgmental words; they did hurt but they won't affect or effect my life because I didn't receive those words and I forgave the speaker; but those words will still happen to the speaker (time is irrelevant).

Is God in Control?

The statement that, "God is in control" has been used so much, especially when things seem to be going wrong. Billy might catch a cold and Harry would say to him, "I'm sorry you got a cold but, ya know, God is in control." So, Harry was telling Billy that God made him sick. Billy's cold turned out to be much worse and he wound up in the hospital needing an operation; Harry still said, "God is in control." Because of the surgery Billy was taken out of work and put on a low paying disability income; but Harry still told him, "God is in control." Harry always preached against borrowing money and having credit cards; he told Billy, "It's a sin to borrow money," but he wasn't offering to help Billy either. Billy's financial situation got so bad that he was driven to borrow some money, and by doing so, sinning in Harry's eyes; Harry still said to him, "Well, God is in control." So evidently, God made Billy sick, cause him to need an operation, caused him to loose his job and go on disability and then caused him to have to borrow money (to sin); of all of these things it is God's desire to have none happen. Now, Harry was saying that God caused all those things to happen to Billy because God is in control. Can you see how ridiculous that is? Either that or, who is Harry's god?

Yes, God is in control when you speak God's Words out of your mouth over the particular situation and put God in control; make God's Words your words. Jesus, God's Word personified (made flesh), said,

> "The words you say will either acquit you or condemn you," (Matthew 12:37 New Living Translation).

Your Words

Notice the first four words in the verse, "THE WORDS *YOU SAY.*" God has spoken great words of health, growth and financial prosperity over you, and that other thing/guy, the rat-face devil, speaks nonsense to you constantly. But you have that awesome choice about whose words you are going to agree with and make your words, and speak.

By your words you either license God to act in your life—each time your situation changes—or you license the false god to take control. If you license God at that particular time then God can control the situation. But if you don't license God and His Holy Spirit then the false god and his unholy spirit will take the initiative and take control of the situation.

2 Timothy 2:24-26 talks about the servant of God not quarreling. But in verse 26 Paul tells Timothy that the devil will do these things at his will. So, let's use that last part in what we're talking about now. If you don't find out and speak God's Words over the situation and put God in control at that particular time then the devil will take control at his will.

In the first paragraph of this section we mentioned Billy and Harry. Billy was born again but he knew nothing about the licensing power of words, well neither did Harry. Harry had always heard that God is in control so that's what he preached, not studying about it first. Harry was content to be a puppet in the hands of his god; but he didn't know that the god he spoke for was not God Almighty. God Almighty was not in control where either of them were concerned. If Billy had never started speaking what he had been speaking and he knew enough to license God in his situations none of that garbage would have happened.

Now, it's just like when a good king makes a law. The king will not break his own law. A person who knows the law but doesn't like it will break the law to get what he wants.

So, to wrap this up, God is in control if you put Him there by your words. But He is a gentleman, he will not stay if you don't want him; if you speak against Him He will leave. As soon as you begin speaking negatively over your situation God will leave because you are speaking against Him (read Malachi 3:13-14). And if God is not controlling your situation then the devil will sweep in at his will and take control of your situation.

Both God and the devil want control of your present situation; but you have the choice of who is going to be in control. The way you put God in control is by your words. If you don't, verbally, give God control of your particular situation then the devil will take control by his/it's own will.

The devil is a thief and a liar, he/it is not honorable, you should know that. If he/it wants something he/it will sweep in and take it if he/it can, if there is nothing stopping him. Your words—copying God's Words— can stop him; you have that awesome ability as a human. So, if you don't give God the control the devil will jump on the opportunity to take it.

Your Words

Chapter 3
Could You Not Hold Your Faith For One Hour?

> "But do not forget this one thing, dear friends: With the Lord a day is like a thousand years, and a thousand years are like a day," (2 Peter 3:8 New International Version).

Allow me to paraphrase, with God's approval, "Don't you know that God's timing is different than yours. With God one day is like one thousand years to you; and one of your days is like one thousand years to God."

When you pray for something you must remember that verse. Do not get uptight if you don't see the results within a day (a day of your time). If one day for God is equivalent to a thousand years for you, then when you prayed 20 years ago and it hasn't manifest yet, you must realize that to God you only prayed for it 40 minutes ago. And already you are about to through away you faith. Well God is asking you; could you not hold your faith for 1 hour?

And if you could hold your faith for 1 hour why would you give up even if it took 2 hours? Hold your faith filled confession for a minute at a time. If 1 minute, go for 2; go all the way up until the manifestation. Of course, we're not saying that God will make you wait but if you have to wait, for 1 reason or another, you should be able to; use patience.

Some Christians that I've talked to have said to me that they don't have patience. Well, either they lied because they are ignorant or they are not really Christians. See, patience is 1 aspect (1 characteristic) of the fruit of Spirit: the fruit of the Spirit is Jesus (love).

So, if those people were, indeed, Christians, then what they were trying to say was that they didn't know how to operate in patience.

> "Knowing this, that the trying of your faith worketh patience," (James 1:3 King James Version).

Patience has the qualities of calmness and continuance, meaning positive confession that what you prayed for is on its way toward manifestation because it is yours.

To tell you the honest truth, if you don't use patience then, aside from it being a miracle, you will never see the results of your prayers. A man can ride his faith like a car but without the use of patience he can't go very far. Patience is the coolant in the engine. You can have the oil, the gas, and have everything else in working order, but if you don't have and use the coolant (your patience) you're not going very far.

Restless Minds

People tend to want results instantly; fast-food restaurants and cafeterias have fostered that idea. Well, most things having to do with the kingdom of God are not instant. Many denominations and denominational people are like this; they pray for something according to their own feelings, or confess for it once or twice, and figure that God doesn't want them to have it because it didn't manifest right away.

Well, come on; use your brain that God so lovingly gave you.

> "You ask and do not receive, because you ask amiss, that you may spend *it* on your pleasures," (James 4:3 New King James Version).

1 very important aspect of the fruit of the Spirit is patience, and 2 meanings of patience are calmness and constancy, the opposites are anxiety (restlessness) and instability.

When you have a need—it's not wrong to pray for yourself, just don't pray lustfully— you must pray according to God's Word and in the name of Jesus. And when you confess something over yourself—and that is not wrong either—do it according to what God had written in Scripture. But, when you pray according to God's Word and in the name of Jesus and in faith you don't need to pray (ask) again for it. What you need to do, for *your* sake, is continually thank God for the answer until it manifests. And when you decide to start confessing positive things over yourself according to Scripture you need to continue to confess those things over yourself until you decide that you don't want them anymore or they had manifested. This exercise has a simple purpose, and it is after you asked God for what you need; the purpose is to remind yourself that you have asked and that it is yours.

Many denominations and denominational people have come up with the idea that God is in control so whatever happens in your life and to you must be the will of God. Let's get down to business; there are 2 families in this universe, the family of God and the family of... man? No, man didn't create; and the devil perverts. Jesus said to the Pharisees that their father was the devil (John 8:44); he's not the creator but the perverter. There are only 2 kingdoms in which you can belong, serve, and be a child of. There is the kingdom of God and there is the kingdom of satan. When God created you He gave you a will and a mouth. It is totally up to you whom you are going to serve, honor and operate under at any given moment. "So, how do I make that decision?" you might ask.

> "Your words will be used to judge you to declare you either innocent or guilty," (Matthew 12:37 Good News Translation).

I've been reading that verse for many years but the other night I got a revelation of it. It's not by someone else's words unless you agree with them and make them your own words. In other words it is what you say over yourself. "But if I'm speaking God's Words then they are God's and not mine," so you would argue. If God speaks something over you and you *don't* repeat it then those words aren't your words, that's true. But, when God speaks something over you—He already had and had it written down—and you agree with it and make those words your own and speak them then you are speaking your own words. Likewise, when the devil speaks something over your life and you repeat them, then you are making them your words and so you are speaking your own words.

The devil speaks death words and God speaks life words.

> "Death and life are in the power of the tongue, and they who indulge in it shall eat the fruit of it [for death or life]," (Proverbs 18:21 Amplified Bible).

So, God is saying through these words of Solomon that the power (authority) to speak the life words of God or the death words of the devil is in your mouth.

But, getting back to the chapter subtitle and the first line, when you speak life words don't expect instant gratification. God is looking for commitment and faith, and that means that He is looking for consistency. So, when you make a positive confession over yourself according to God's Word you are going to have to be consistent; keep doing it or it might not manifest.

Ross has been confessing his healing for his eyes for years. Every day, before he would put his glasses on in the morning, he would confess, "I can read and see without glasses." He is in his later 40's and everyone says that the older you get the worse your eyes get and if you have a prescription they can only get worse. But Ross's eyes are, indeed, getting better. In fact, the last 2 times that he went to the optometrist he was prescribed a weaker prescription, this happen twice within a year. Does God love Ross more than you? Absolutely not! But Ross is putting what he has learned about the positive confession according to God's Word into operation and is committed to continuing it. I know Ross personally, so I know that this is the truth. At this rate Ross will be without glasses in a few years.

Your Words

Chapter 4
Treating And Speaking to Others

> "Treat others as you want them to treat you. This is what the Law and the Prophets are all about," (Matthew 7:12 New King James Version).

This is saying that if you don't want people to do bad things to you then don't do bad things to others. Suppose you need people to help you do something. Well, are you helping others to do what they need help doing? If you get involved and help them then, according to this verse, someone will come and help you.

This is interesting, but hardly anyone has ever though of that verse as a monetary verse. Someone might say, "I never thought of that but when people do bad things to me I tend to hurt them back." Well, hurting someone because they have hurt you is not walking in love. But, no, I never thought of that verse in a monetary way either. However, it does fall in line with Luke 6:38,

> "Give, and it will be given to you. A good measure, pressed down, shaken together and running over, will be poured into your lap. For with the measure you use, it will be measured to you," (New International Version).

Now, Jesus explained that verse, Matthew 7:12, in more specifics. He said,

> "A second is equally important: 'Love your neighbor as yourself,'" (Matthew 22:39 New Living Translation).

Jesus was talking about the greatest commandment, and then He said that to love your neighbor as yourself is as important as loving God. You may scoff at that and say, "No it isn't;" but other versions say that this second one is like the first. So, what would you say and/or do to yourself? Well, when you are saying or doing something to someone else, Jesus said, you're saying that or doing that to yourself. I know that's hard to figure but that is what Jesus was saying when He told you to love them as, or the way, you love yourself.

When I was in college a girl walked up to me and told me that she was a Christian. She said, "I love everyone but I hate myself." Now, what does that tell you? I could tell that she was having self-esteem issues because of all the razor scars on her wrists. I didn't doubt that she honestly put her faith in Jesus but she did have those issues that she needed to get help with. She could not love everyone else and hate herself because that goes against what Jesus said in Matthew 22:39.

> Jesus said, "Words are powerful; take them seriously. Words can be your salvation. Words can also be your damnation," (Matthew 12:37 The Message).

Paul speaks on this same line in Romans 10:10 when he tells you that,

> "and it is by confessing with your mouth that you are saved" (part 'b' New Living Translation).

But, as for Matthew 12:37, some versions will tell you whose words will be your salvation or damnation; the New Living Translations says,

"The words you say will
either acquit you or condemn you,"

many other versions have it this way too. I've had someone speak negative words over me before as most of you have also, I'm sure. I've got good news for you and bad news for them. Those words that they said to you don't have to have any effect on you; just don't receive them, don't repeat them. But those bad words that they spoke will have an effect on them; they said them.

They had just demonstrated their love for you and that means that they had just demonstrated their love for themselves. "Love others as you love yourself." If a man will love himself the way God loves him and tells him to love himself—not being prideful—then he wouldn't be speaking those negative words over himself. And when he is speaking those negative, hurtful words over you—his own brother or sister—he is speaking those words over himself. I know, ouch!

What Did David Throw?

> "Then David put his hand in his bag and took out a stone; and he slung *it* and struck the Philistine in his forehead, so that the stone sank into his forehead, and he fell on his face to the earth," (1 Samuel 17:49 New King James Version).

Was it the stone that threw Goliath off his feet and killed him? Well, if you will read the previous verses you may see what it was that killed Goliath. That stone that David used to knock that big bully down was more than just a stone; it was a catalyst of his faith. Goliath was a moving target. Do you know how hard it is to aim a sling at one small spot on a large moving target? I would say, extremely. In fact, it's next to impossible.

So, it was David's faith that knocked that belligerent, big, dishonorable, bully off his feet and killed him. "No, it wasn't. It was the Word," you're getting smarter. To be sure, it was David's love for his God that brought him to that point of what he did. And it was his faith in the Word that took Goliath out. Now, look at why I say that.

> "David answered, 'You are coming against me with sword, spear, and javelin, but I come against you in the name of the Lord Almighty, the God of the Israelite armies, which you have defied,'" (1 Samuel 17:45 Good News Translation).

So, it was the Word of God, but it was also David's words of his faith. You're probably thinking, as some might, *'If it was God's Word how did it become David's words?'* That's a good question. Now, are you ready for *the* good answer? Jesus said,

> "For by your words you will be justified, and by your words you will be condemned," (Matthew 12:37 New King James Version).

David put God's Word in his mouth and said it.

See, whatever words you speak become your words when you speak them. "But so-n-so said them," someone might say. Yes, and when you repeated them they became your words. That is why many people, in the past at least, used to jump on you for saying something negative about yourself. Well, the fact that they would jump on you, *so-to-speak*, was not the correct way to handle things; but correction was necessary. God puts out positive words and the

46

devil puts out negative words; so, you have a choice of which words you are going to make your words. That means that you choose whose words you are going to agree with; you agree with them by speaking them and making them your words.

> "You poisonous snakes! How can you evil people say anything good? Your mouth says what comes from inside you. Good people do the good things that are in them. But evil people do the evil things that are in them. I can guarantee that on judgment day people will have to give an account of every careless word they say. By your words you will be declared innocent, or by your words you will be declared guilty," (Matthew 12:34-37 GOD'S WORD Translation).

A person will become evil (not good) or good depending upon the words that that person listens to and pays attention to. If you listen to evil junk continuously, or on the majority, and pay attention to it you are going to turn out to be an evil person, speaking trash and cursing. If you listen to words from God's Word continuously, or on the majority, and pay attention to them you will become a good person. And the words that go in will eventually come out, if allowed, and that's when they become your words. Either those words that come out of your mouth are good or they are bad; and that is what you will be judged for in the day of manifestation (judgment).

So anyway, Goliath called himself a dog (1 Samuel 17:43) (devilish words), essentially barking at David to try and kill him. His day of manifestation came fast and David essentially said, "Okay, you asked for it." Then THWACK!!

Chapter 5
Words Affect Lives

"By your words you will be declared innocent, or by your words you will be declared guilty," (Matthew 12:37 GOD'S WORD Translation).

When a woman says something about herself she is actually making a confession, and when she is confessing that over herself she is making a judgment call about the one who created her.

A man might have said something positive out of God's written Word once or twice and figured, *'Well, that doesn't work,'* because he did it once or twice and gave up. He didn't give it a chance to work and he went back into his old routine of speaking along with what the world says. He really doesn't notice that what he has been saying in agreement with the world has been affecting and having an effect on the way he lives his life and things concerning his own body on a daily basis. The reason that he doesn't notice this is because it seems to be norm; everywhere he looks people are talking the same way and the same kind of things are happening to them; that only makes sense. And when approached with a message about positive confessions he says, "I don't believe in all that confession stuff; it doesn't work anyway." He just doesn't realize that confessions have been working in his life all along, only in reverse because he has been confessing the negative. Or he might say, "Well, I tried that positive confession stuff several years ago. Yeah, I did it twice but nothing happened." So, he went back to agreeing with the negative stuff of the world, run by the devil, and he doesn't realize it but those confessions have been working.

God created mankind—men, women and children. He recreated the born again Christian but He created all of mankind in the beginning; actually, He created all life.

Jim is a great artist and he painted a masterpiece, assessed to be worth over

$44,000,000. Along comes Jake who looks on the picture with disgust and he says, "This painting sucks worms." If you were Jim and that was said about your creation what would you do?

George is a sculptor who is celebrated as the top sculptor in world (the best). His sculptures are priceless. Fred sees one of George's master sculptures and spits on it; he tells his friends that this guy, George, doesn't know art. George also makes clothes and does art on clothes. George creates and makes everything that man needs to live. After Fred cusses out George's sculpture he looks at his clothes and finds that George created them too. This embarrasses Fred. Then Fred goes home and finds that this same George made everything that he owns. If you were Fred what would you do? George overheard everything that Fred said—about the sculpture, about his clothes, about everything. So what would your response be if you were George?

God is the master sculptor in life and celebrated all around. His art and sculptures are beyond priceless. What is different about these sculptures is that they move and talk and think for themselves. Fred is one of those sculptures.

But Fred doesn't like something that he does so he begins putting himself down. Many others agree with Fred and soon it is common to speak negatively about oneself. But, who created Fred and who created you? Fred was spitting on himself because of something he was doing; that didn't stop Fred from doing what he was doing. But when Fred was putting himself down— being a creation of God—he was also putting down the one who created him.

And one of those who were in agreement with what Fred was saying, because it seemed the norm, was talking like Fred for decades. Then this sculpture meets another sculpture that tells him how God wants him to speak. He tries it a few times but goes back to speaking like Fred because it is the norm and, "that confessing positive doesn't work," also the fact that change is hard. Well, it's been working positively for those who had made a determined effort to start it years ago.

Confessing the negative works and people do that without even thinking about what they are doing. In fact, the devil will see to it that when people confess the negative the results of their confession will come to pass fast. It takes no faith and no patience; it's the easiest thing in the world to confess the negative because "everyone's doing it." But now, try to turn around the negative confession and the results of the negative confession. It's not too easy but it can be done.

Confession works whether for the good or bad. If you had gotten into a habit of determinedly confessing God's Word over yourself—you may have to stick with it for years before you ever see anything—the manifestation will come. On the other hand, if you had been confessing along with the status queue, which is most likely the devil's words, they will come to pass faster.

Now, suppose you had been talking in agreement with the status queue for 19 years and then stopped; you didn't really turn to a positive confession, you just stopped the negative confession. You still aren't confessing the positive over yourself but you aren't actively confessing the negative over yourself either. And it still seems that everything that happens to you is more toward the negative. Well, there is a good reason for that; actually, there is more than one good reason. Reason #1) other people may be continually confessing the negative over you and you haven't built a verbal wall to keep the negative out. Reason #2) when you were speaking negatively you were planting weeds, weeds have deep extended roots. You can't simply stop watering a weed and have it die; you must dig it up or it will come back.

When you, as a born again Christian (a new creation), make the confession that you are still a sinner that is born again you are judging God (your creator) to be very bad at His work. You're saying that God doesn't know the difference between a sinner and a saint. I wouldn't do that if I were you. I really don't think God appreciates that very much.

The Word of God says,

> "This was to fulfill what was spoken by the prophet Isaiah: 'He took our illnesses and bore our diseases,'" (Matthew 8:17 English Standard Version).

There are many Scriptures that tell you, the twenty-first century Christian, that healing is promised; it's your for the... asking? No, *thanking*. So, when you say, over and over, that you are sick and *hope* to be healed by the doctor or medicine you are spitting in your creator's eye. It's a statement of unbelief, meaning you don't believe in or for the healing given to you by Jesus because it's not *already* manifest and some symptoms of a cold are on you.

You cough and you think that you're catching a cold; so you say it and say it and now you got it; your confession worked. It might have just been a speck of dust that got into your throat but now you got a cold because you called for it. Don't tell me confession doesn't work. Just turn it around and begin to confess the positive—according to God's Word—and then continue to confess the positive.

Read, Speak, Repeat

People who don't believe that daily confessions of the positive have any effect either haven't done anything about it or have tried it a few times and given up because they hadn't seen anything. There is 1 thing that those people have in common in their use of positive confession, no commitment to their confession. They just aren't committed to holding on to their positive confession until it manifests in their lives.

Look at an example: Jack had been speaking along the same declining ways of the world for 40 years. He felt a tickle in his throat; it made him want to cough. Well, the first thing that came to his thoughts was that he was catching a cold or something worse. So, naturally he began speaking that because he was taught in church that you have to speak it if you feel it. He went to a doctor who told him that he had a bad disease; so he began confessing that he had this disease. He did that because the doctor said that and, after all, doctors know everything about health.

When Jack was 45 he met a guy who taught him about the positive confession. So, Jack tried it once or twice and then went back to speaking and complaining about the problem. Finally, after 55 years Jack died of that bad disease.

> "Words are powerful; take them seriously. Words can be your salvation. Words can also be your damnation," (Matthew 12:37 The Message).

Where was Jack's commitment? Why didn't the positive speaking work for him? Why did he die? Was it the positive confession that killed him?

Your Words

Jack spent 40-45 years, actually 55 years, speaking the negative just like the world's system, less 2 times with the positive confession of health. Let's figure that out; let's say that each day he speaks negatively over himself once: 55 years = 20088 days, less 2. So, Jack confessed 20086 negatives over himself (must have wanted it pretty bad). But he only confessed the positive 2 times. You do the math. How much is 20086 negatives-2 positives? So, where was Jack's commitment? I'm sure, positive, that in 55 years Jack spoke the negative over himself more than once a day; I'd venture to say that if he was like most people he spoke negatively over himself twice – ten times each day. So, we can change that 20086 times to anywhere from 40172 times to 200860 times, minus 2 positives. Now, what's that tell you? Does the phrase, 'Elephant against a gnat' mean anything to you?

When you read something in God's written Word that will have a positive effect on your life, and you confess it once, you really don't have any right to expect the manifested change right away, if ever. Why is that? Because, saying it once shows very little, if any, conviction or commitment. How long have you been repeating, and believing, possibly, what the world as been saying, before *and* after your good confession?

Suppose you had grown up for 25 years speaking in agreement with what the world says. Then you saw it in the Bible that God said,

> "But he was wounded for our transgressions, he was bruised for our iniquities; the chastisement of our peace was upon him, and with his stripes we are healed," (Isaiah 53:5 Darby Translation)

So you read that and confessed out loud once, "I am healed by Jesus' stripes." You are now 50 years old and you are dying with cancer. Someone preaches about the power of the positive confession of God's Word. You tell that person, later, that you don't believe in that because... and you tell that person why. Well, is it any wonder why you don't believe it? You don't believe it because no one ever taught you that in order to make it work you must be committed to it until the end.

> "And Saul said, Who are You, Lord? And He said, I am Jesus, Whom you are persecuting. It is dangerous and it will turn out badly for you to keep kicking against the goad [to offer vain and perilous resistance]," (Acts 9:5 Amplified Bible).

The King James Version says, "it is hard for thee to kick against the pricks." Yes, it was hard for Paul to go against the tide of Christianity at that time; but it is also hard for Christians to make positive confessions against a world of negative confessions, as is the way of the world. In grade school you were counted as an outcast if you didn't have the same sneakers as everyone else.

You would come home and say to your folks, "I need these sneakers, I'll die if I don't get them."

Your mom would say to you, "Honey, we just got you some great sneakers."

Your dad might add, "We can't afford to get you more new sneakers."

You would then complain, "But, everyone's got them. Oh, come on. What, do you want me to be the laughing stock of the world?"

Well, it goes something like that. If everyone you knew, everyone in your church group, jumped off the Empire State Building would you do it too? People are all telling you to do it because, "everyone's doing it." Are you going to also? It's very dangerous and it might kill you (probably will). No, you'd better not.

Do you recall the parable of the sower? Jesus was talking about many things in that 1 parable; most Christians hadn't gotten it all yet, they just look at it as a lesson about the hundred-fold return. But the seed that is received on stony ground grows fast and dies off. This is because of a lack of commitment. These people received it with joy and started well, we can say they started with their good positive confession of God's Word. But because of no fellowship in the Word, no one came to help them, and they saw no results of their confessing the positives over themselves they stopped.

Some people of some *denominations* don't agree with positive confessions based on God's Word because they can't see it before they confess it. "After all," they say, "if you can't see it why talk about it as though it's there." When I first spoke of my computer—I had already prayed for it—and thanked God for it, my friend asked me, "Do you need a computer?" to which I answered, not another one. See, Romans 4:17 says that God called things that were not there as though they were, and Abraham imitated (believed) God. In other words, Abraham (representative of the believer) did what God did, and he spoke what didn't appear as though it was. I have never been without a computer since soon after that, because I continue in my confessions of the positive from God's Word. I didn't wait until I had a computer on my desk before I began confessing for a computer. But if I only confessed that I had it once and didn't see it manifest right away and stopped; would the computer ever have manifest? Probably not. I would have probably had to have gone to the store and bought 1. But these computers were given to me because I didn't give up. But I will stay with computers all my life because I confess it and repeatedly continue.

What you confess on a daily basis, even what you continually confess on any basis, is probably what you want. Oh, you may not think you want it and you may declare that you don't want it, but the fact that because you keep confessing it just might prove otherwise.

Most people, whether Christians or not, think that their mouth is connected to their mind and what they say has nothing to do with their lives. But your mouth *is* connected to your heart (the core, control center of your body, your spirit) and what you say has everything to do with your life, your body, and your financial status. That is why Jesus said,

> "The good man brings good things out of the good stored up in his heart, and the evil man brings evil things out of the evil stored up in his heart. For out of the overflow of his heart his mouth speaks," (Luke 6:45 New International Version).

And that is also why many preachers and I say that we can tell what's in your heart simply by listening to you talk for an hour; but you have to start and hold the conversation.

Chapter 6
You Choose

"Words kill, words give life; they're either poison or fruit—you choose," (Proverbs 18:21 The Message).

You choose what you are going to say. You might have heard someone speak negative, sloppy words and then, when you bring up the subject, they answer, "Well, they made me say that." That's not true; nobody can make anybody say anything negative or positive. For example: If Sam is a good man and has been trained to speak good things, then Jake cannot, no way, make Sam curse him or curse someone else. Sam chose the words that he spoke. Jake may have said, "Sam, I want you to say_____ (whatever)," but Sam always has a choice. If the choice is curse your wife or be killed, Sam could always choose death. That choice might just send Sam to heaven early but it's his choice.

> "What you say can preserve life or destroy it; so you must accept the consequences of your words," (Proverbs 18:21 Good News Translation).

In other words, you will live by what you say; your words will come back on you. People want to prosper in their lives, financially, heath wise, socially, and spiritually. But something has to happen first, before prosperity comes on them. They must first say what they want to come on them.

> "As it is written: 'I have made you a father of many nations.' He is our father in the sight of God, in whom he believed—the God who gives life to the dead and calls into being things that were not," (Romans 4:17 New International Version).

According to Jesus, in John 14:12, the word **believe** holds the connotation of doing, or copying. Abraham believed God. And what greater honor is given God than for someone to do the same as Him? So, Abram must have said what God said about him; when God called him a father of many nations, that's what **Abraham** means, he must have done the same thing. Abram said, "I am Abraham." I tell you, if there had been a legal system there and then like there is in American today his name would have been on file as Abram, unless he got it legally changed. But he still called himself Abraham, because God called him Abraham, before he had 1 child, and he was over 75 years of age.

God has said some things over and about you, and the devil has also said some things over and about you and still tries to get you to repeat them. But no matter how hard he/it tries and threatens your life, he/it cannot make you say anything that you don't want to say. And, much to your chagrin, God can't either. Many of you would like Him to, and some even think He can, but He gave you that awesome ability and right of choice.

Simple visual aid:

←---The devil puts out words--,--God puts out words--→

-------(put your name here) chooses the words--------

By Your Words

"For by your words you will be justified and acquitted, and by your words you will be condemned and sentenced," (Matthew 12:37 Amplified Bible).

That is a loud statement, not just because it is from a loud Bible (the Amplified Bible) but it is also a deep truth.

There are 5 words that I want you to see, most people run right over these 5 words when reading this verse and pay very little attention to them. The words are, "by YOUR words you WILL." The Holy Spirit brought this to me so I started praying about it and listening to the Holy Spirit. Notice, Jesus did *not* say, "by your neighbor's words you..." and He also did not say, "by your words you might..." no, that's too iffy. He also did not say, and this is something to watch for, "by your words you will, *only when you speak your words over yourself*..." He also did not say, "by *My* words your will..."

Jesus was very specific when He said this, He did not mince words. So, the words that *you* speak, whether spoken over yourself *or others*, are the words that will justify or condemn you.

Think about this: There is only a little written about the life of Jesus. But, how long did Jesus live on the Earth? 33.5 years, approximately. Right, and does the little that is written about His life cover everything. No, but it does cover what we need to know about Him and His teaching. That's true, but it's not all covered in depth. For instance; Jesus talked about the Holy Spirit more than 80 times; things about the Holy Spirit are in the New Testament at least 198 times, from John the Baptist to John the Beloved.

Just so, words were 1 of Jesus favorite subjects, He talked about words to everyone He talked to or talked to Him. And the issue wasn't simply words in general but the specific words of the person that He was talking to or the person who was talking to Him. People called Him all kinds of names; so he just told them that, "by your words you will be justified and acquitted, and by your words you will be condemned and sentenced." They were condemning themselves while thinking that they were doing God a favor.

Your Words

We have 2 people, James and John. John does something inadvertently that James gets mad at. John apologizes to James and repents but James says something harsh to John, calls him a derogatory name. John forgives James for doing that and does not repeat those words. Now, who if anyone is going to reap the results of those harsh words and that name-calling? If you answered, "James," you're right. Obviously, James did not think about his words and spoke out of anger, and now James is going to reap condemnation because of those words. If he repents of those words maybe, just maybe, those words will not affect him or have an effect on him; but there are no guarantees about that.

You've heard the child's phrase, "What you say bounces off me and sticks to you." That phrase was thought of as just a statement said in defense to someone who was calling a kid ugly names; adults thought it was false but it is actually a Biblical phrase. You might throw your words as arrows at other people but those arrows are actually boomerangs and they will come back on you, whether they affect the other person or not.

Chapter 7
It Takes Faith

The main reason why people don't keep up with the positive confession is because they don't see the manifestation of their new confession within 1 week. Usually they are looking for the results of their positive confession right away, as in the first day.

I had someone ask me why it took so long; she said, "Why is it that when I read something in God's Word and I begin confessing it over myself, I don't see any results?"

Well, she will see the results if she doesn't give up the confession.

> "So let's not get tired of
> doing what is good. At just the right

time we will reap a harvest of blessing
if we don't give up," (Galatians 6:9
New Living Translation).

If she will stick with it, no matter what happens, she will get the desired results—maybe not her desire but God's desire. Another reason people don't stick with positive confessions is because; it's a 2-part reason; 1) they have been confessing their circumstances and the negative for how ever old they are, and 2) it takes faith; the longer it takes for their confession to manifest, the stronger their faith must be.

"And without faith it is
impossible to please God, because
anyone who comes to him must believe
that he exists and that he rewards those
who earnestly seek him," (Hebrews
11:6 New International Version).

Trying the positive confession doesn't work; no one is going to speak the negative circumstances over themselves for thirty years then change their whole life and every circumstance to the positive by making a positive confession once or twice.

Now, for corrective confessions, confessing the positive to correct a negative that was brought on because of anything—because of surgery, negative living, and negative confessing all your life, all that stuff. You need to pray according to God's Word first.

> "We have courage in God's presence, because we are sure that he hears us if we ask him for anything that is according to his will," (1 John 5:14 Good News Translation).

So, when you ask in prayer—**prayer** meaning communication—according to what is written in God's Word you can have faith that you have the results.

> "And if we know that he hears us—whatever we ask—we know that we have what we asked of him," (1 John 5:15 New International Version).

Now, once you have prayed according to God's Word—I like to quote His Word—you can boldly and with faith make that positive confession. And if you will keep standing with your faith filled words you will see the results in... I don't know how long. For me, some things have manifested in a few days and other things have taken a few years *and* others are still in the faith stage. I'm still confessing for them, but I won't give up.

Be Patient With Me

When you begin speaking the positive confession, whether over yourself or over others, you will be tempted to quit. Why is this? Well, it's because speaking positive things, speaking things that don't seem to be happening... that's not normal. But now, look at what God, your creator and the One whom you should believe did (Abraham believed Him).

> "As it is written: 'I have made you a father of many nations.' He is our father in the sight of God, in whom he believed—the God who gives life to the dead and calls into being things that were not," (Romans 4:17 New International Version).

Abraham believed God; so what did he do? He did like God because to believe strongly means to copy, he started calling himself a father of many nations, that's what **Abraham** means. How long did Abraham have to speak that he had the first son before it happened (talking about Isaac, his promised son)?

If Abraham, the father of those who are full of faith, had to speak things that be not as though they were, what makes you think that this is something that you don't have to do? When Abraham started doing this he was 75 years old, Isaac was born when he was 100 or more years old. He had to speak things that appeared not as though they were for at least 25 years. He implemented patience and stuck with it... even though it made him look silly.

Patience means to be steadfast, to stick with the good that you had started until you see the results. It may take your whole life to see the manifestation but stick with it and you will.

Your Words

Chapter 8
Within the Four Walls

Many people will do these things and don't have too much difficulty... within their church group. What I mean by their church group is the people they hang around, other 'Christians' of like faith, those who believe the same way they do, their denomination. But those same people who have no problem doing these things in their church group do have a problem doing these same things when they are among other people who aren't part of their church group, or by themselves.

> "But I say unto you, Love your enemies, bless them that curse you, do good to them that hate you, and pray for them which despitefully use

you, and persecute you," (Matthew
5:44 King James Version).

Those of your church group are most
likely not your enemies, those who will curse
you, those who hate you, those who will
despitefully use you, or those who persecute
you. **Love** includes speaking good things to and
over and about, speaking things into existence
(Romans 4:17), and doing good things for
(Matthew 7:12). **Bless** means to speak good
things to, over and about among other things.
And **pray for** includes speaking and doing (if
necessary).

> "But you will receive power
> when the Holy Spirit comes on you;
> and you will be my witnesses in
> Jerusalem, and in all Judea and
> Samaria, and to the ends of the earth,"
> (Acts 1:8 New International Version).

Change the word **witnesses** to the word
representatives and read that again. Jesus
wants us to represent Him to a lost and dying
world. Now, what is a representative?
Wouldn't you think a representative should
speak and act just like the 1 that he or she is
representing? A representative of the army,
navy, air force, or marines is called a G.I. Joe; a
Joe means his name isn't what's important, he is
a government representative, a government
issue. The American ambassador represents

America wherever he or she goes. When people attack him or her they are attacking America because he or she *is*, in essence, America.

Well, you and I are supposed to be representatives of Jesus, we are supposed to be, in essence, Jesus to everyone around us. Wherever we go we should speak and do just like Jesus did and does.

There is the phrase that has become popular among 'Christians,' it asks what would Jesus do? It is a Biblical question to ask and some 'Christians' actually ask it in most situations. I like to go beyond that question and do what Jesus would do.

So, Jesus is looking for representatives to go out into the highways and hedges and "be a Jesus" to everyone, not just to other representatives within your church group. When an acquaintance or a stranger *or a rival* says something negative to you, whether about you, themselves, or about someone else you should respond by saying something positive. Because, whether they know it or not, they are speaking about themselves all the time; in so doing they are speaking about the One who created them. And you, when you are responding you are speaking about yourself and in so doing you are speaking about your creator.

A real *Christ*ian is a Christian outside of his or her church group, not simply a Christian in his or her comfort zone.

Additional Books by Winner

Simply The Facts

Your Heart is an Open Book

A Pocket Full of Wisdom

When You Finally Get to Later, It's Too Late!

The Echo Effect

The Great Chess Game

Harvest

White Clothes

Please write to me and I will be more than happy to pray for you; and *if you would like* I can email or send you some information that may help you.

Please fill out and use the bottom of this page with your initial correspondence.

Bread of Life Int. Min.
P.O. Box 222
Little River, KS 67457

Your first name_____
    Last name_____

Mailing Address_____
    City_____

State/Province_____
    Country_____
    Zip Code_____

Phone # where we can reach you_____
Your email
address_____

Any specific prayer requests or praise
report_____
_____
_____
_____
_____
_____
_____(If you
need to use the other side of the page, go for it.)

It is the goal of this ministry to spread God's pure love and His Word correctly until the end comes.